THE BEST OF

2005

MATTHEW PRITCHETT studied at St Martin's School of Art in London and first saw himself published in the *New Statesman* during one of its rare lapses from high seriousness. He has been the *Daily Telegraph*'s front-page pocket cartoonist since 1988. In 1995, 1996 and 1999 he was the winner of the Cartoon Arts Trust Award and in 1991 and 2004 he was 'What the Papers Say' Cartoonist of the Year. In 1996, 1998 and 2000 he was *UK Press Gazette* Cartoonist of the Year and in 2002 he received an MBE.

The Daily Telegraph

THE BEST OF

2005

'We're going to have
to shoot the staff'

ORION

An Orion paperback

First published in Great Britain in 2005 by
Orion Books
A division of the Orion Publishing Group Ltd
Orion House
5 Upper St Martin's Lane
London WC2H 9EA

1 3 5 7 9 10 8 6 4 2

© 2005 Telegraph Group Limited

The right of Matthew Pritchett to be identified as the
author of this work has been asserted by him in accordance
with the Copyright, Designs and Patents Act, 1988

A CIP catalogue record for this book
is available from the British Library

ISBN 0 75286 485 8

Printed and bound in Great Britain by
Butler and Tanner Ltd,

www.orionbooks.co.uk

THE BEST OF

*'There's never an iceberg
around when you want one'*

General Election

General Election

General Election

'I like the negative personal attacks but all the policy stuff turns me off'

'Take from the rich and give to the poor? Oh hell, we're Liberal Democrats'

General Election

'There isn't a train –
there isn't even a pledge
about a train'

'It doesn't generate any
electricity but it keeps the
candidates away'

General Election

'My integrity has become
an election issue'

'My lawyer has advised me
not to vote'

General Election

'In a poll, 92% of politicians said that the voters were a bunch of two-faced liars'

General Election

'Still undecided?'

'I think 3,000 postal votes would look very suspicious'

Meanwhile in Rome …

General Election

'Look, that bit over there is drying'

'I fooled everyone – I didn't vote tactically'

General Election

The Tories

Howard says he'll go …

The Tories

'Excuse me, can you spare a few moments to lead the Conservative party?'

'Can George come out and join the shadow cabinet?'

The young shadow chancellor

Law and Order

Law and Order

'We use the blue lights and siren to get away from danger as quickly as possible'

'Do you sell gift vouchers for paying spot fines?'

Law and Order

'Pointing a finger and shouting
"Peeow" can hardly be described
as having a replica weapon'

Law and Order

Law and Order

'People under house arrest go out more often than we do'

'You bought that dress? I thought you were wearing it as part of a community service punishment'

Law and Order

'You're just wearing that so you can't come to the shops with me'

'All I said was, "Not one of your best sermons, vicar"'

Law and Order

'Someone stole my identity and all my friends and colleagues like him better than me'

'I think the dog wants a walk'

Intruders

'I heard a noise downstairs, quick, pass me my reading glasses'

'Let's invite your family for Christmas'

Intruders

'No, that was just reasonable force, THIS is grossly disproportionate'

'Sorry . . . I thought you were an intruder'

Ukraine Elections

US Elections

'Gentlemen, before the healing,
a little more gloating'

The Labour Party

'The Blair-Brown feud has only been going on for seven years; we've been married for more than 20'

'Darling, you said you were ready to go; there is nothing that you could ever say to me now that I could ever believe'

The Labour Party

'Waste? . . . Cutbacks?'

'No, not your vote, I'm asking
if you have any old receipts'

Dubious expenses

Nannygate

'Somebody close to
Mr Blunkett must be selling
stories to the press'

'Tell the nanny I'll buy her a
car, but I'm not having an
affair just to get her a visa'

Nannygate

'We'll never see
David Blunkett'

'I just hope none of this
intrusive material appears
on his ID card'

Nannygate

'Fast-track a leaving card'

'I wanted to go to see
Blunkett the Musical
but I'm under house arrest'

Sven

The Hunting Ban

'Instead of hunting foxes
we'll be allowed to secretly
brief against them'

The Hunting Ban

'That lot are merely weekend rioters'

The Hunting Ban

'STOP! I've got silk stockings and I'm not afraid to use them'

Attack on The House

The Hunting Ban

'Well, this is awkward...'

The Environment

'The washable nappy has really hit the wind farm this time'

'Does this milk smell off to you?'

The Weather

'All that chaos at Heathrow –
aren't you glad we didn't
go abroad?'

Rain ...

'I'll take the high road
and end up on the low road
afore ye ...'

... and landslides

Terror

Terror

War Aftermath

'And I got this one for saying sorry afterwards'

Army Cuts

'Right, men, when I give the order, I want you to desert'

Health Scares

Health Scares

'We're snowed in – the one who draws the short straw has to eat the Worcester sauce crisps'

'If this isn't legal justification for the war, I don't know what is'

MRSA

'I'm a superbug'

'Would you mind if some
student cleaners watched me
mop up under your bed?'

Schools

'Put your pens down, children, the exam system has just changed again'

'In the good old days we failed all our A-levels'

Schools

Road Charges

'I'm charging you £1.34 for every mile we drive in the wrong direction'

'This is a toll motorway, would sir like to borrow a jacket and tie?'

The Royals

Harry's costume

The Royals

That wedding …

The Royals

'A METEORITE! And it's heading straight for Windsor register office'

What more could go wrong?

Pensions and Inheritance

'There is a £57 billion pension gap – I'd start hiding nuts if I were you'

'I'll wash your go-cart for £2'

Pensions and Inheritance

'If anything should happen
to me, I don't want a
sage and onion stuffing'

'Your accountant's written
"Do not resuscitate"
on your notes'

Incapacity

'I live in almost constant benefit . . . I mean pain'

'Sail a ship? Are you out of your mind?'

We aren't sailing

'A girl in every port?
That's not saying much'

'It's a wonderful cruise – I
usually get terribly homesick'

Ellen MacArthur

Gypsies

'It's a way of life – my people have been building conservatories without planning permission for generations'

And finally ...

'I always say, putting money into a pension fund is a mug's game'

'There's been a misunderstanding, I said change the oil, not bail out the company'

And finally ...

And finally …

Scotland bans smoking

And finally . . .

And finally . . .

Inspection of London

'I don't want to use alarmist rhetoric, but we must do something about our borders'

And finally . . .

'Hello, I want the phone
number of a better
directory enquiries service'

'It's paternity leave, stop
calling it house arrest'

And finally . . .

'Higgins, the headmaster would like a word'

'Would you like legal aid with that?'

School uniform row

And finally . . .

And finally . . .

'And that's another one
of me not decommissioning
my weapons'

'Thanks for coming in.
Could either of your children
work our computer?'

And finally . . .

'A lottery ticket and,
to hell with the odds, I'll have
a first class stamp as well'

'I've been doing
a dozen for £1.59'

And finally . . .

'Oh do cheer up! It's like being married to Hugh Grant'

Gloomy Hugh

And finally . . .

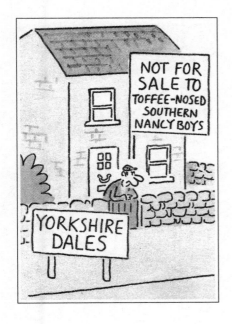

'We've got a gusher'

Shell profits

And finally . . .

'Could passengers on the lower decks see if we've landed yet'

Super jumbo

'Hi, honey, I'm home'

Crash landing

And finally . . .

'Shouldn't we be boycotting
South African goods until
Mark Thatcher is free?'

'Hello, you're through to
Norwich Union . . .'

And finally . . .

'I'm going to knit a jumper
for our grandson'

And finally . . .

'This is the last time
I come to Glastonbury'

And finally . . .

'I don't want Bob Geldof to know I'm missing Live 8'

And finally . . .

'He claims he cares about world poverty but he doesn't do much swearing'

'Could you end world poverty a little more quietly?'

Live 8

And finally . . .

'My wristband says, "Make Britain's rebate history"'

'The EU farm subsidies are NOT, I repeat NOT, up for negotiation'

And finally . . .

'Yes, I'll be a long time,
I'm reviewing the fleet'

'OH NO, Hardy,
I've lost my ID card'

And finally . . .

'I reversed all the way to work and I was sent a cheque for £28.52'